Introduction

Once the hunting preserve of kings the Forest today is a vast leisure centre covering 148 square miles where people live, work and enjoy many outdoor pursuits like camping, walking, cycling and riding. A recent recommendation to grant National Park status will ensure its future.

Administration of the Forest is the responsibility of The Verderers Court, the second oldest in the land, who sit at Queens House, Lyndhurst. They control and administer the "Rights of Common" and appoint 4 agisters who oversee the welfare of the Commoners' animals.

Apart from 30,000 acres of woodland, vast areas of open heath, grass lands, bogs or valley mires and gorse occupy a further 93,000 acres which make walking an interesting varied experience.

The ten walks listed in this book, which range from $3\frac{1}{2}$ miles to $7\frac{1}{2}$ miles, offer a diversity of interest from woodland nature reserves, riverside paths and open heath to historic monuments, towns, villages and popular pubs.

© Power Publications
1 Clayford Avenue
Ferndown
Dorset. BH22 9PQ

ISBN 1 898073 19 8

Other local publications

Pub Walks in The New Forest
Pub Walks in Hampshire & the IOW
A Mountain Bike Guide to the Highways & Bridleways of Hampshire & The New Forest

Publisher's note

Whilst every care has been taken to ensure that all the information contained in this book is correct neither the authors or publishers can accept any responsibility for any inaccuracies that occur.

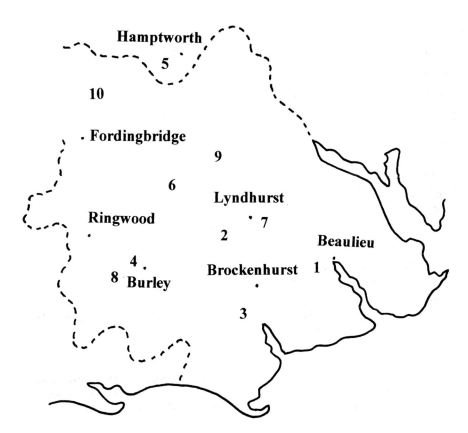

Beaulieu & Bucklers Hard

Beaulieu village is situated on the B3054 between Lymington and Hythe. There is a car park in the centre of the village behind the garage, no charge on Sunday, weekdays presently 50p for 4 hours.

Approximate distance: 3½ miles. OS maps: Landranger 196, Outdoor Leisure 22. 386/023.

Beaulieu famous for its abbey ruins and the National Motor Museum, has remained unspoilt, despite its many visitors. This short but delightful walk follows the Solent Way to the charming village of Bucklers Hard, a former naval ship-building yard in the 18th century (Nelson's fleet was built here), that nestles beside the picturesque Beaulieu River. The village has a fascinating little maritime museum which recalls this tradition and cottage display recreate 18th century life. Part of the return route winds through woodland along a delightful riverside path. Otherwise the walk retraces the scenic outward journey. It is easy going underfoot and ideal for the whole family.

From the car park turn right into the village, go past the very historic Montagu Arms and take the waymarked footpath on the right (Solent Way). Continue along the gravel track to a stile beside a gate. Keep to the well waymarked route ahead, with views across the Beaulieu River past a small inlet and along the left-hand edge of a field. Eventually reach a house and a track and keep ahead, soon to bear right and then take the track left, signed Bucklers Hard.

Remain on this long and straight path through woodland. At a small car park, follow the gravel track right and shortly pass boatyards to reach the quay at Bucklers Hard. Having explored this attractive village return to the small car park on the edge of the village. Bear right onto a pleasant path that winds its way through the woodland, over tiny bridges and beside the tidal river. Eventually you will reach the main path close to the house passed on the outward leg. Turn right and retrace your steps back to the village.

Park

Bucklers Hard

Bucklers Hard

Palace House

Bolderwood & the Knightwood Oak

Bolderwood is best reached from the A35 at the turning for the Ornamental Drive (approximately 2 miles) but can also be reached from Lyndhurst through Emery Down. Large free car park.

Approximate distance: $6\frac{1}{2}$ miles. OS maps: Landranger 195, Outdoor Leisure 22. 242/087.

Although a little demanding especially in the winter when conditions underfoot can be very wet this is essentially a very enjoyable walk on differing tracks and paths leading first to the deer viewing platform then down through attractive forest to Bratley Water and on towards the Knightwood Oak, one of the oldest in the Forest. The route back is similar.

Leave the car park heading south, cross the road to the small wooden gate opposite and walk down to the deer viewing platform where, if lucky you can expect to see sika, roe, fallow and red deer. Walk away from the platform down the path to the track, turn left and then right by the three-ringed post.

Follow this narrow track down through the trees and further on fork right by the memorial stone, cross the gravel track and continue through the trees to the half wooden gate then follow the track ahead marked with red ringed posts.

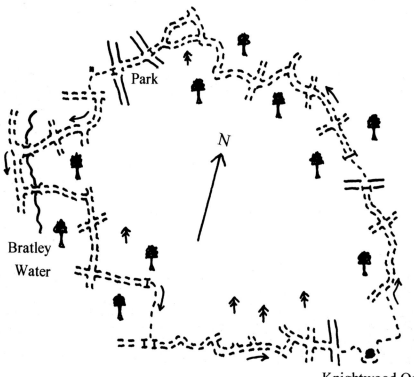

Park

N

Bratley
Water

Knightwood Oak

Walk No. 2

Cross Bratley Water and turn left, then left again over the small bridge climbing the path to the track turning right. Walk for a while past the first cross track turning left at the next one. This sometimes muddy grass track leads to a wide wooden gate. Pass through and turn right onto this not very well defined path as it twists its way through the trees. Maintain direction fairly close to the boundary on the right. Soon passing an area fenced on both sides before reaching a cross track.

Go through the gate on the left and follow this wide twisting track for some distance until you reach a narrow grass track on the right. Follow through to the gravel track and turn left. Walk past the gravel track on the left, up the rise and fork right. Turn left at the next track junction then go right onto the very wide gravel track, over the cross track, up to the road and turn right.

Cross over, enter the car park and join the footpath signed for the Knightwood Oak. This magnificent pollarded tree is over three hundred years old and one of the oldest in the Forest. Walk round to the rear of the tree and follow the little path into the trees, up to the wire fence and turn left. Wind your way through the trees then turn right upon reaching the track.

Ignore all side turnings until you reach the gate. Cross the road and bearing slightly left walk through the trees and up to the small gate. Follow the path/track ahead, go straight ahead at the cross track, over the next cross track and further fork right following the marked cycle way track ahead. Proceed up and round eventually turning left at the grass track which rises to meet the main track and gate at the top; alternatively for firmer ground keep to the track ahead then fork left up to the car park at the top.

The Knightwood Oak

Walk No. 3
Boldre & Roydon Wood Nature Reserve

From the A337 Lyndhurst to Lymington road turn off at Battramsley Cross signed to Shirley Holms and Sway. Park in the Shirley Holms car park signposted on the left after the railway arch.

Approximate distance: 6 miles. OS maps: Landranger 196, Outdoor Leisure 22. 298/984.

An enjoyable walk at first along peaceful forest roads leading to Boldre thereafter on woodland paths and tracks passing through Roydon Wood Nature Reserve. Apart from the occasional damp spot the going is generally good underfoot. Spring is a good time when the bluebells are at their best.

Leave the car park towards the heath and turn left along the gravel track. Ignore the side paths but keep walking as the track narrows and reaches dwellings on the left. Turn left into the lane then right. Pass under the railway bridge and continue walking until you reach the main road.

Carefully cross over turning right then next left. The lane descends gently eventually reaching the Red Lion at Boldre, a nice old pub worth a visit. Keep straight ahead over the bridge and turn left into Rodlease Lane. After rising from the brook take the track on the right, footpath signposted. Walk up to the road and straight across onto the wide gravel track opposite.

Continue past the farm buildings and just beyond the turning for Little Dilton Farm take the signed bridleway track on the left, which leads to the very attractive Roydon Wood Nature Reserve. Covering an area of 150 acres the woods are home to birds, reptiles, 29 species of butterfly and many wild flowers including bluebells. Two trees to be found are the wild service tree and long leafed lungwort both national rarities. The narrow track threads its way between mature deciduous trees eventually reaching a cross track at which point turn left, cross the Lymington River, join the track beyond the gates and turn left.

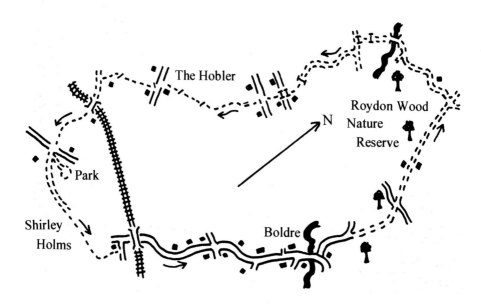

Further ahead look for the narrow signed bridleway on the right. Very pretty and uneven underfoot this narrow path twists its way through the trees (Fluder's Clump) up to a track. Keep straight ahead through the wide forest gate, across the grass, out through the gate on the far side and walk over the road to the kissing gate opposite.

Go down the narrow path to the lane and straight across to the path opposite leading to a bridge. Walk through an area of wet grassland, up to the stile and into the field. Keeping close to the boundary make your way to the stile at the top and follow the shaded path ahead up to the main road turning left.

Walk as far as The Hobler another very popular and interesting pub definitely worth a visit. Carefully cross the road to the stile beside the dwelling and proceed along the narrow path leading to the Forest. Bear left along the track beside the dwellings to reach the wide cross track (a short diversion to the right will bring you to the model boating lake) then turn left and further on fork right over the railway bridge and take the little path on the right over the brook. A gentle climb up the hillside opposite in line with the overhead cables leads directly to the car park.

The Hobler

Walk No. 3

The Lymington River

Fluder's Clump

Burley, Burley Street & Moor

Burley lies halfway between the A31 and A35 south east of Ringwood. Park in Castle Hill car park signed to the west of Burley Street on the road to Crow.

Approximate distance: 5½ miles. OS maps: Landranger 195, Outdoor Leisure 22. 198/038

Burley is one of the most picturesque and most visited villages in The New Forest consisting of gift shops, tea rooms and a famous pub, The Queen's Head. The walk follows a track to a view point over Cranes Moor before descending to the road to pick up forest paths leading to Burley. The return route is by way of tracks and paths through Burley Lawn and across Burley Moor to Burley Street. Although not over demanding the forest paths can be very muddy in the winter.

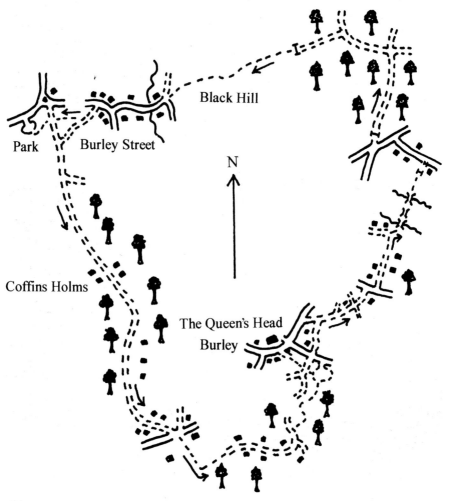

From the rear of the car park follow one of the narrow paths up the hillside, join the track and turn right. Further on fork right following it past the fort viewpoint. When you eventually reach the road cross over and join the wide and often muddy track opposite. Keep straight ahead for awhile and then bear left up the rise following the twisting path through the trees keeping as close as possible to the boundary of the property on the left. Beyond the half forest gate join the track which descends past several dwellings. After passing the track on the right and few steps later join the small path on the right then fork left at the cross paths walking up through the trees to the car park at the top.

To visit Burley turn left, cross the drive way of Moorhill House Hotel to the half forest gate and take the path on the left which leads directly to the centre of the village opposite The Queen's Head, a good refreshment stop.

Retrace your steps back up to the car park then cross the road to the sports ground following the track, past the school turning right at the church and keep to the main track before finally turning right in to the lane.

In fifty yards take the track on the left which passes beside The New Forest Badger Watch. At the end of the track keep straight ahead across the lawn to the far side turning immediately right in front of the dwelling. Take the narrow path, which runs close to the boundary of the property following it as best you can leading to a small bridge and stile. Keep straight ahead to a similar bridge then go up beside the boundary to a large wooden bridge over the river. Keep to the narrow fenced path, over a crossing point and across a small field to a gate then follow the track up to the gate turning left into the road.

Turn left at the junction then immediately right into South Oakley Inclosure. Take the first wide track on the left then the next grass track on the left. Leave by the gate and follow the path ahead, over a small stream eventually dipping towards the dwelling and lane. Keep straight ahead across the ford, then right through Burley Street and, after passing the Post Office turn left up Randells Lane. Climb the stony track and after passing the large white house on the left bear right over the green to pick up the path through the trees finally crossing the track down the path to the car park.

Burley

Walk No. 4

Queen's Head

Hamptworth & Langley Wood Nature Reserve

Village signed from the B3079 at Landford. Park opposite the Cuckoo Inn. This delightful thatched inn is one of my personal favourites, totally unspoilt serving beautifully kept real ales and moderately priced bar meals.

Approximate distance: 5 miles. OS maps: Landranger 184, Outdoor Leisure 22. 243/198.

A very enjoyable and interesting walk at first along a peaceful country lane after which track and field paths guide you to Langley Wood Nature Reserve. The best time is April onwards especially when the bluebells are at their best and conditions are generally good underfoot but do expect the occasional wet area.

From the inn turn left then first right into Lyburn Road signposted, to Nomansland. Follow the lane round to the right turning right at the next bend. A few dwellings line this peaceful country lane, which rises towards Home Farm. Continue ahead down the track into the woods. Good at first the surface soon deteriorates and narrows before reaching the tarred lane and the settlement. Wild flowers include snowdrops and bluebells.

Just before reaching a black and white timbered house look for a short gravel track on the right leading to a stile signposted, to Langley Wood. Walk down between the fenced fields, go through the trees and across the grass to the bridge (can be wet) then straight ahead beside the hedge and up the field to the road at the top.

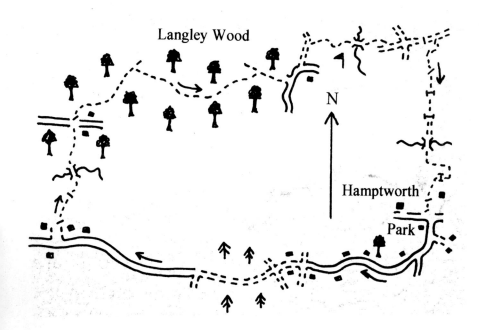

Walk No. 5

Cross to the stile opposite and enter Langley Wood Nature Reserve. This ancient wood is rich in wildlife including lichens, mosses, woodland plants, insects and birds and five species of deer. Of special interest is the small leafed lime once common in the forests of Southern England. Keep to the well-trodden path ahead forking right at the first path junction (waymarked). Follow this well signed path to the fingerpost then turn left into an area of coppiced hazel and large oaks above a carpet of bluebells. Further on cross the ditch and keep to the signed path ahead until you reach the cross track at which point turn right then left into the lane.

In just a short distance take the track on the left, re-enter Langley Wood and further on fork right down the gully, path way-marked. Just before reaching the golf course look for the little signed path on the left which descends through a thicket to a bridge then up between the trees to join the rising gravel track. At the cross track keep straight ahead up to the farm, through the gate and across the yard.

Almost immediately look for a stile on the right and, keeping close to the hedge walk a short distance to the stile, along the narrow path climbing into the field. Cross to the kissing gate in the opposite hedge and maintain direction to the far side of the field. Follow the woodland track down to the bridge, up into the field, presently a nursery, and straight across to the hedge on the far side turning left. Turn right at the corner and almost immediately pass through the gate into the field on the right. Walk down to the stile in the fence, across two more before turning right into the road back to the pub.

The Cuckoo Inn

Langley Wood

Linwood & High Corner

There are two routes to Linwood. From the A35 take the Bolderwood Ornamental Drive, go under the A31 and fork left at the road junction. Alternatively from Ringwood leave the A338, Fordingbridge road at Ellingham. Park in Appleslade Inclosure just before reaching the Red Shoot Inn.

Approximate distance: $4\frac{1}{2}$ miles. OS maps: Landranger 195, Outdoor Leisure 22. 185/094.

A very enjoyable walk along forest tracks and field paths which takes you across Linford Brook and down to the popular High Corner Inn.

Head into the forest and almost immediately bear left through the half gate and up the track. At the top of the rise turn left following the track up to, and into, a small clearing. Turn right and, in fifty paces look for a narrow grass track on the left, which passes beside a sweet chestnut tree. Follow it steadily downhill through fairly deep shade, forking right near the bottom. Make your way past the lily pond to the track and turn left over the wooden bridge.

The gravel track swings to the left arriving at a forest gate. Enter the inclosure walking for some distance and, having past the track on the right take the next track on the left. Grass covered and damp in places it rises steadily between oak trees to meet a gravel track. Cross to the grass track opposite and walk down to meet the gravel track at the bottom.

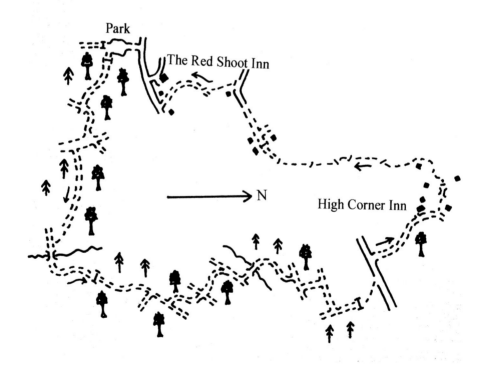

Turn right and then next left, over the bridge and up to the cross track following the marked cycle track to the right then almost immediately turn left up the wide grass track. Turn right onto the narrow path at the top then next left up to the gate and crossing point. Keep to the narrow path ahead, cross the road turning left then take the gravel drive on the right which descends to the High Corner Inn. (Conveniently open all day in summer).

Carry on down the track and very soon go left over the verge and across the small field to the signed footpath. It circumvents several properties before reaching a path between fenced fields. Climb the stile at the bottom and proceed to the stile opposite maintaining direction to a stile beside a gate. Cross to the stile on the left and go up the field eventually reaching the narrow grass path, which leads down to a stile and gate.

Follow the track ahead and, after passing the dwelling on the left, climb the stile into the field on the left. Follow the hedge line round to another stile then up the narrow track, past the dwelling onto the driveway and round to the road turning right. Divert to the right for refreshment at the Red Shoot otherwise continue along the road back to the start.

High Corner Inn

The Red Shoot

21

Lyndhurst

Lyndhurst is the capital of the Forest with a superb museum and visitor centre. Situated at the junction of the A337 and A35 it is also the headquarters of The Forestry Commission. Park in the Swan Green car park located south of the village a short distance up the Emery Down road.

Approximate distance: 5½ miles. OS maps: Landranger 196 & 195, Outdoor Leisure 22. 288/289.

An extremely enjoyable ramble which completely circumvents Lyndhurst. Forest paths lead to the little hamlet of Bank after which more tracks and paths eventually bring you out onto the Beaulieu road. After crossing open moorland and skirting a golf club you reach Pikeshill and Emery Down. Although not over demanding at times some areas can be very wet and muddy.

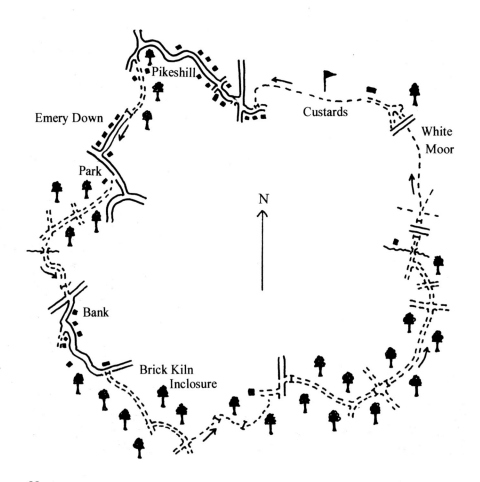

From the car park cross the Green bearing right but just before reaching the corner by the road turn right and climb the beaten track through the trees. Go over the cross path and down the track ahead to the cross track at the bottom. Turn left towards the open area of grass, cross the small concrete bridge and keep straight ahead following the track which bears left up through the trees to a stile beside a gate.

Carefully cross the busy A35, go down the lane to Bank and fork left at The Oak Inn, a very good refreshment stop. Follow the lane through the village until you reach the first gate on the right opposite the large dwelling signposted, to Brockenhurst. Take the second proper track on the left then left again at the cross track bearing left across the open grass making for the small gate to the inclosure. Follow the gently rising path and then turn right into the bluebell wood. Upon reaching the gate turn left onto the well-beaten track. Further on cross the driveway to the school and make for the exit point a little way along the fence.

Carefully cross the road to the track and gate opposite. Further on turn left, leave by the forest gate turning right onto the wide track and almost immediately go left through the deer gate. Stay on this attrac-

tive grass covered track keeping straight ahead at the cross track after which it bears left. Upon reaching the track junction turn right, cross the little brook and walk up to the Beaulieu road.

Go straight across to the half gate and up the rise to meet the track at the top. Ignore the sandy track straight ahead instead fork left down the moor towards the distant traffic keeping as best you can to this ill-defined path which eventually reaches the underpass. On the far side of the A35 bear left onto the tarred drive leading to the golf club. Continue ahead, past the club house, along the grass until nearing the road at which point join the narrow path off to the left. Cross the small bridge, leave by the little gate in front of the dwellings and turn right up to the main road.

Turning right carefully cross over and take the turning on the left into Pikes Hill. Go past the Waterloo Arms, another good refreshment stop, and follow the lane ahead past all the dwellings, up to the road junction and turn left. Almost immediately join the gravel track on the left. This lovely bridleway rises steadily to a cul-de-sac. Walk up to the road, cross over turning left back to the car park.

Ringwood, Hightown & Kingston Common

The easiest route to the start of this walk is to turn off the A31 at Picket Post then take the first right at Burley Street. Leave your car in Vales Moor car park, which is on the right.

Approximate distance: $7\frac{1}{2}$ miles. OS maps: Landranger 195, Outdoor Leisure 22. 187/040.

An enjoyable walk around the ancient market town of Ringwood. After crossing an area of Strodgemoor Bottom peaceful lanes and a public footpath guide you to Sandford and then along a bridleway to Kingston. An attractive footpaths takes you onto Kingston North Common with the option of further exploration. The return route is via Upper Kingston and Crow with the opportunity to visit the Owl Sanctuary. Housing the largest collection of owls in Europe, the sanctuary is open daily, March to November from 10am to 5pm. In the winter only at weekends and the Christmas holiday. Informative lectures for all age groups take place every day at 11 am and 2 pm. An interesting network of public footpaths guide you back beside an attractive lake and past some handsome properties.

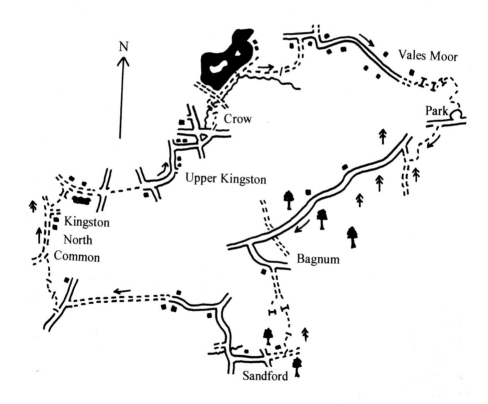

Turn right out of the car park and, just before reaching the yellow-ringed 40-MPH signs on the road, take the path on the left down through the trees then left onto a wider track. Further on fork right up to the track, straight on past the dwelling on the left and turn left into the forest road.

Follow this peaceful rural lane for just over a mile and beyond the dis-used railway line take the next left towards Bagnum Riding Stables. Just past Rose Cottage join the signposted footpath on the right which leads to two farm gates. Pass through the one on the left and keep beside the hedge until you reach the stile, then negotiate the narrow path up to the track and turn right walking as far as the road.

Bearing right cross over into the lane opposite, turn right at the junction, over the bridge walking along the lane until you reach Brixey Farm. Take the next left, go past the dwelling, keeping to the wide gravel bridleway which leading to the main road.

Carefully cross over turning left, climb the stile onto the Avon Valley Path and bear right in the direction of the waymark arrow. Two more stiles and you reach a grass path leading to a large wooden platform stile. Go out onto the track and turn right. After passing the dwellings fork right across the grass, over the track and straight ahead keeping to the Avon Valley Path. Cross the little bridge and turn right onto the gravel track walking until you reach the road again.

Carefully cross to the signposted path opposite and make for the lane on the far side of the field. Keep straight ahead and then bear left into Green Lane. Walk for awhile and then turn right into Streets Lane. Upon reaching the road cross over, go up to the junction and straight across to the stile. (To visit the Owl Sanctuary turn left, left again and then right). Walk round to the stile and bridge, cross into the field on the left, turn right to the stile then keep straight ahead on the very attractive path beside the lake.

On the far side keep straight ahead towards the dwellings but before reaching the stile ahead of you turn right to the stile often concealed in undergrowth. Pick up this little fenced path which leads to a field, bear left following the marked path up to the stile in the top left-hand corner and turn right up the track to the lane.

Turn right keeping to the lane which bears right and then left, meanders for a while past several dwelling before reaching the entrance to a fine dwelling. This is a permissive path allowing us access to the Forest by the generosity of the owners. Walk up the drive and bear right upon reaching the grass, cross to the gate on the left, walk up the fenced path to the next gate finally passing through the little gate onto the moor.

Pick up the little path ahead, which eventually rises to a track, then turn right and almost immediately go up the narrow path on the left. Precise directions back to the car park can be difficult due to many animal paths but as it is only a short distance down to the road you will soon locate the car park. After taking a path over the hill you will reach a wide track, if you turn left then look for a small path on the right it will bring you directly back to the car park.

Hightown Lake

Walk No. 9

Rufus Stone & Minstead

The turning from Rufus Stone is signposted off the eastern carriageway of the A31 a short distance before Cadnam. The alternative route is to come off the B3079 at Brook and follow the signs for Upper Canterton. Park in the Sir Walter Tyrrell car park.

Approximate distance: 5½ miles. OS maps: Landranger 195, Outdoor Leisure 22. 270/125.

An interesting walk commencing at the Rufus Stone, an iron monument marking the spot where, it is said, William II (son of the Conqueror) was killed by an arrow. Paths and forest tracks across open grazing land and through dense forest ultimately bring you to Minstead and the Trusty Servant, a convenient half way stop. Whilst here take time to visit the 12th century church, famous for its three-decker pulpit and wooden galleries, one even has its own fireplace. To the rear of the graveyard lies the body of Conan Doyle the creator of Sherlock Holmes. Peaceful lanes, woodland paths and tracks guide you back to the start. Furzey Gardens, which occupies eight acres of delightful, informal gardens, is open daily from 10am – 5pm.

Walk along the verge to the pub and, bearing right cross the green opposite keeping close to the inclosure on the right. Follow the path (not very clear) which leads to Coalmeer Gutter. Cross on the improvised block bridge to the track opposite and in about fifty paces, having crossed the ditch turn right onto the grass strip. After a number of wooden crossing points, keep straight ahead on the grass between the inclosures walking as far as the golf course then bear left down to the plank bridge. Walk away from the course, up to meet the track on the right following to the road.

Turn right, cross by the ford and take the next track on the left by the post box (bridleway signposted). Turn right at the cross track, walk past all the dwellings and bear left across the grass towards the trees. As there is no defined path try and keep to as

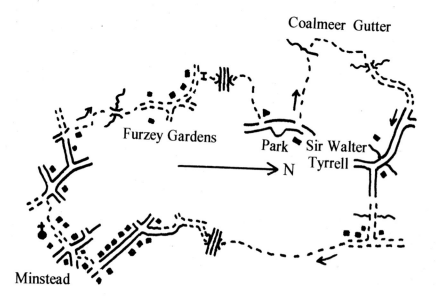

Coalmeer Gutter

Furzey Gardens

Park • Sir Walter Tyrrell

⟶ N

Minstead

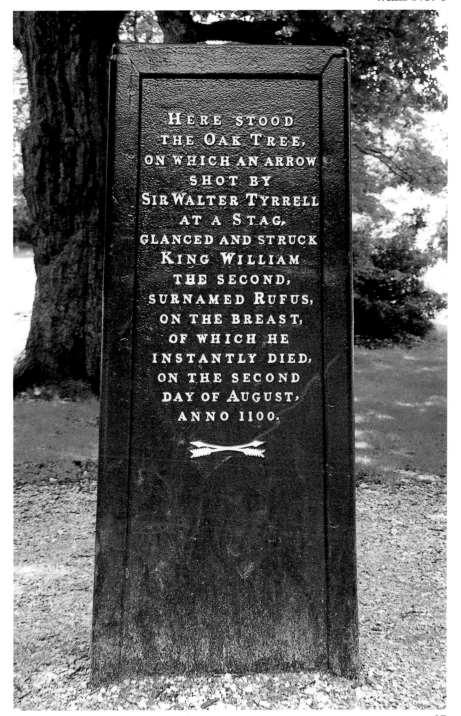

HERE STOOD
THE OAK TREE,
ON WHICH AN ARROW
SHOT BY
SIR WALTER TYRRELL
AT A STAG,
GLANCED AND STRUCK
KING WILLIAM
THE SECOND,
SURNAMED RUFUS,
ON THE BREAST,
OF WHICH HE
INSTANTLY DIED,
ON THE SECOND
DAY OF AUGUST,
ANNO 1100.

Walk No. 9

straight a line as possible all the time heading south picking up the occasional pony track around the trees. You will know when you are near the road by the increase in noise. Eventually you will reach a track and the underpass.

On the far side turn right up the short track then continue up the road towards Minstead turning left into Seamans Lane. Walk past all the cottages then go right into Bull Lane and almost immediately join the signed footpath on the right. Home to many primroses and bluebells it takes you down to the centre of the village. Pass in front of the Trusty Servant pub, or rest awhile, continue up the lane to the church then join the path on the right.

At the bottom cross the road and go up the lane opposite leading to Furzey Gardens, take the next left walking until you reach the stile on the right, footpath signposted. Follow it down to the stream and up to the wood turning immediately right after the stile. Cross the board walk to the path opposite and further on take the path on the right bringing you out by Furzey Gardens.

Take the grass centred track opposite and continue up the lane/track and turn left onto the wider track by the dwellings. After passing the new cottage go through the gate on the right, down to the underpass then bear right across the grass to meet the track. Just before reaching the road there is a small path on the left which leads directly down to Rufus Stone and the car park.

Trusty Servant Inn

Minstead Church

Woodgreen

Village signed off the A338 Fordingbridge to Salisbury road at Breamore. Turn right in the village then right again into Castle Hill. Park at the viewpoint.

Approximate distance: $3\frac{1}{2}$ miles OS maps: Landranger 184, Outdoor Leisure 22. 170/166.

Woodgreen was once famous for its cherry orchards, now long gone but few people outside the village are aware of the beautiful murals in the village hall, painted in 1932/3 by two London artists. Funded by the Carnegie Trust they depict village life. (Viewing is by prior appointment only: telephone Mrs Windall (01725) 512529). The friendly family run pub is a local gem with open fires, real ales and excellent home-cooked food. My walk is easy going on field and forest paths, tracks and peaceful country lanes, perfect for an autumn day.

Cross to the forest gate opposite and turn right following the well-beaten path between mature chestnut and other deciduous trees. Keep straight ahead until you reach the cross track then turn left, go up to the gate and cross the road to the gate opposite. Ignoring all side turnings follow the track ahead through the forest which eventually leads to the road.

Keep straight ahead to the track opposite following the well signed path up to the stile, across the field to the stile opposite, join the track and turn right. (For a slightly shorter walk you can turn left). Take the signed bridleway on the left following the track to the right of the dwelling and shortly join the signed footpath on the left which descends gently between rhododendron bushes, the

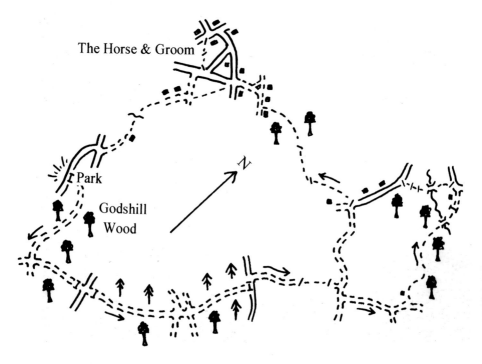

path marked at intervals with yellow circles painted on the occasional tree. After descending to a small bridge go through the gate and up the field beside the hedge to a similar gate, past the cottage and out to the lane.

Almost immediately climb the stile into the field on the left and go down beside the hedge, cross the bridge at the bottom and head up the ill-defined path through the trees. Three stiles later turn left into the lane.

Walk until you reach the entrance to the dwelling then cross the stile on the right. Proceed on the well-beaten path across the meadow to the stile from which point you have a good view of Hale Park. Turn right down the field to the stile; bear left down through the trees and up to the lane.

Turn right then next left. Upon reaching the green keep straight ahead making for the house and gravel track beyond but for refreshment divert right down the lane to the Horse & Groom. Leave the pub turning left and go up the footpath at the side, across the green at the top and turn right by the dwelling onto the gravel track. After passing some lovely thatched cottages the grass path dips towards the stream. Thread your way up between the trees opposite turning right around the cemetery and down the entrance to the road. Cross into Castle Hill opposite walking the short distance back to the viewpoint.

Castle Hill

31

The Horse & Groom

The Green